Skills in English

Level 3

Writing

Terry Phillips

Garnet
EDUCATION

Published by
Garnet Publishing Ltd.
8 Southern Court
South Street
Reading RG1 4QS, UK

ISBN 1 85964 793 6

British Library Cataloguing-in-Publication Data
A catalogue record for this book is available from the British Library.

Production

Project manager:	Richard Peacock
Editorial team:	Nicky Platt, Lucy Thompson
Art director:	David Rose
Design:	Mark Slader
Illustration:	Beehive Illustration/Roger Wade Walker, Karen Rose, David Stevens
Photography:	Apple Computers, Inc., Corbis/Bettmann/ Hulton-Deutsch Collection/ The Scotsman/Underwood & Underwood, Digital Vision, Image Source, Photodisc

Garnet Publishing wishes to thank the following for their assistance in the development of this project:
Dr Abdullah Al Khanbashi, Abderrazak Ben Hamida, Maxine Gillway, Susan Boylan and the Level 3 team at UGRU, UAE University

Every effort has been made to trace the copyright holders and we apologize in advance for any unintentional omissions. We will be happy to insert the appropriate acknowledgements in any subsequent editions.

Printed and bound
in Lebanon by International Press

Skills in
English
Writing
Level 3

Contents

Book Map

Theme	Input text types	Output text types	Writing skills
1 Education, What's Your Learning Style?	Rules and examples	Advisory text	• Revision
2 Daily Life, What Made Me … Me?	Magazine article	Factual article	• Concluding opinions • Writing about famous people
3 Work and Business, Hiring and Firing	Flow charts	Description from a flow chart	• Using the passive to describe a process
4 Science and Nature, Heating and Cooling	Magazine article, diagrams and tables	Factual article	• Joining sentences with *because, so, if* and *to*
5 The Physical World, Extraction Industries	Magazine article, diagrams and tables	Factual article	• Joining sentences with *which*
6 Culture and Civilization, The Civilization Still Flourishes	Essay	Essay	• Joining sentences with participles • Joining sentences with *who*
7 They Made Our World, Labour-Saving Devices	Essay	Essay	• Using demonstratives for textual reference • Talking about obligation in the past
8 Art and Literature, Novelists and Their Novels	Essay	Essay	• Joining sentences with *when* and *where* • Joining sentences with *because of*
9 Sports and Leisure, As Figure 1 Shows …	Essay, graphs and charts	Essay	• Displaying statistics • Joining sentences with *since* • Describing graphs and charts
10 Nutrition and Health, Education for Everybody	Graphs, tables, charts and mini-texts	Essay	• Revision

Introduction

THIS COURSE IS THE WRITING COMPONENT of Level 3 of the *Skills in English* series. The series takes students in four levels from Lower Intermediate to Advanced in the four skills, Listening, Speaking, Reading and Writing.

In addition, there is a remedial/false beginner course, *Starting Skills*, for students who are not ready to begin Level 1.

The writing component at each level is designed to build skills that help students survive in an academic institution where written assignments are wholly or partly in English.

This component can be studied on its own or with one or more of the other components, e.g., Listening and Reading.

The course is organised into themes, e.g., *Science and Nature, Art and Literature*. The same theme is used across the four skills. If, therefore, you are studying two or more components, the vocabulary and structures that you learn or practise in one component will be useful in another component.

Within each theme there are four lessons:

Lesson 1: *Vocabulary*
In the first lesson, you revise words from the theme that you have probably learnt already. You also learn some new words that you need to understand the texts in the rest of the theme.

Lesson 2: *Writing*
In this lesson, you practise skills that you have learnt in previous themes.

Lesson 3: *Learning new skills*
In this lesson, you learn one or more new skills to help you with writing.

Lesson 4: *Applying new skills*
In the final lesson, you use your new skills with another writing text. In most cases, the texts in Lessons 2 and 4 have a similar structure, so you can check that your skills have improved.

In this theme you are going to write about your experience of learning English and your preferred style.

Lesson 1: Vocabulary

You are going to learn some vocabulary you need to talk about your experience and to give your opinion.

Ⓐ Read the advice.
   1 Find the correct red word for each space, but don't write it.
   2 Cover the red words. Can you remember how to spell the missing words?
   3 Check your answers with the red words.

doubled *(adj)*

link *(v)*

multiple *(adj)*

open *(adj)*

organise *(v)*

practice *(n)*

relevant *(adj)*

revise *(v)*

silent *(adj)*

function *(n)*

grammar *(n)*

language *(n)*

listening *(n)*

pronunciation *(n)*

reading *(n)*

speaking *(n)*

vocabulary *(n)*

writing *(n)*

Advice to students

- When you are learning new words, always underline _____ consonants or vowels (e.g., *ski__ll__, cho__oo__se*) and _____ letters (e.g., *know*) to help you notice and remember.
- You need lots of _____ of writing a new word. Write it out 10 times.
- You should always _____ before a test. _____ your notes in a logical way and read through the _____ sections – the ones you need for the test – several times.
- There are two main kinds of test – _____-choice questions (e.g., *Choose A, B or C*) and _____ questions (e.g., *Where do you live?*).
- Remember to _____ short sentences to make longer, more interesting sentences.

Ⓑ In this theme, you are going to talk about rules in language learning. Which area of language learning does each rule come from? Cover the green words. Write the answers in the grid to reveal the key word. Then uncover the green words and check your spelling.
   1 We can use many verbs as nouns.
   2 'Hi!' is an informal way of saying 'Hello'.
   3 Always use a capital letter at the start of a sentence.
   4 We make the past tense of regular verbs with the base + *ed*.
   5 We often use 'I'm sorry' when we are apologising.
   6 The letter *s* in the word *is* sounds like /z/.
   7 We often scan or look quickly at a text first.
   8 Try to hear the key information – don't worry about the grammar at first.

Hi, John!

1										
2										
3										
4										
5										
6										
7										
8										

Ⓒ Write another rule from each area of language learning.

Lesson 2: Writing

Ⓐ What kind of a learner are you? Do these exercises and find out.

1 You must learn some spelling rules for the present simple tense. Look at the example words – Extract 1 (opposite). Work out the patterns, then complete the blue table.

2 You must learn some spelling rules for the present continuous tense. Look at the rules – Extract 2 (opposite). Complete the green table on the right.

Ⓑ What is the main difference between Exercise A1 and Exercise A2?

1 Discuss in pairs.

2 Read the text in the yellow box and check your ideas.

3 Which kind of a learner are you?

Ⓒ If you think you are an inductive learner, look at Extract 3. Do the tasks. If you think you are a deductive learner, look at Extract 4. Do the tasks.

Ⓓ Exchange texts with a person who did the other set of tasks. Explain your tasks and check your partner's work.

infinitive	3rd-person singular
mix	
push	
study	
miss	
go	
try	
pay	

infinitive	*ing* form
put	
die	
try	
send	
read	
run	
lie	

Are you an inductive learner or a deductive learner? Inductive learners prefer to look at examples and work out the rules. Deductive learners prefer to look at rules and work out examples. If you preferred Exercise A1, you are probably an inductive learner. If you preferred Exercise A2, you are probably a deductive learner.

Lesson 3: Checking skills

Ⓐ Read this English assignment.

> What kind of a learner are you? Write about your experience of learning English, your reasons for learning and your current level. Then say if you are an inductive or deductive learner. Give reasons for your opinion.

1 What information must you include in your answer? Make a list of points.

2 Turn your list into a table for recording your notes.

Ⓑ Read this answer.

1 Divide the text into four paragraphs.

2 Make notes about this learner in your table from Exercise A.

Ⓒ Make another copy of the table from Exercise A. Make notes with true information about you.

Ⓓ This answer needs an introduction. What should the writer include in this paragraph?

I have been studying English for 10 years. I started learning when I was eight and I'm 18 now. We do about 100 hours each year at school, so I have studied for about 1,000 hours in total. I have never been to Britain or the States, but I use my English quite a lot in my own country. I sometimes need it in shops, and I sometimes have conversations with British and American people. I am learning English for several reasons. Firstly, I want to be an English teacher. Secondly, I want to study in Britain or the States. I think that I need a good level of English to get a place at a university abroad. I believe that I am now at Higher Intermediate level. I am quite good at reading, but my speaking is better. I am not very good at writing. In fact, it's my worst skill. I need to work hard in this area. I think I am an inductive learner. I don't like learning grammar rules or pronunciation rules. I prefer to look at texts or examples and work out the rules. In my opinion, you learn English better when you read a lot and listen a lot. I don't like doing lots of grammar exercises and I hate listening and repeating all the time.

Extract 1

infinitive	3rd-person singular
sit	sits
read	reads
wash	washes
fax	faxes
pass	passes
teach	teaches
do	does
fly	flies
carry	carries
say	says
buy	buys

Extract 2

Add *ing* to the infinitive **except** ...

if the infinitive ends:

1 in an e, take off the e and add *ing*.

2 in ie, change the ie to y and add **ing**.

3 in a consonant, then a vowel, then a consonant (CVC), double the final consonant (=CVCC*ing*).

Extract 3

Task 1 Match one example below to each rule opposite.
- *I like music.*
- *I am living with a friend at the moment.*
- *I am reading this example.*
- *I start work at 7.00 every day.*
- *I work in a bank.*

Task 2 Write a short text about yourself. Try to include at least one example of each rule.

The present simple vs the present continuous / progressive

We use the **present simple** to talk about:

a situations – job, home, family.

b routines – things that we do all the time.

c thoughts, feelings, emotions.

We use the **present continuous** to talk about:

a current actions – things that are happening at the moment.

b current situations – things that are true for a short period of time.

Extract 4

Task 1 Read the text.

1 Underline all the verbs in the **present simple** tense.

2 Circle all the verbs in the **present continuous** tense.

Task 2 Make some rules for using each tense.
Example: *We use the present simple to talk about jobs, e.g., He works in a large park.*

Task 3 Write a short text about yourself, using the present simple and the present continuous.

This is John Smith. John is a gardener. He works in a large park in the centre of the town. He works from Monday to Saturday. He starts work every day at 7.00. He finishes at 4.00. He doesn't work on Sundays. John loves trees and flowers. He enjoys working in the fresh air. He doesn't like offices or factories. John wears the same old clothes every day – an old green jacket and a brown hat. He doesn't like wearing suits and ties.

It is Monday today, but John is not working. He is lying in bed. He isn't wearing his green jacket and his old hat today. He is wearing pyjamas. He is ill. He doesn't want to be in bed. He wants to be outside, with the trees and the flowers.

Lesson 4: Applying skills

A Read the text in the yellow box. Then look at Task 1 or Task 2.

> If you are an inductive learner, you can often see patterns when you are reading. Then you can use the patterns when you are writing. If you are a deductive learner, you need to learn rules. Then you can apply the rules when you are writing.

Task 1: For inductive learners
Find and underline verb patterns in this section of the text from Lesson 3.

I have been studying English for 10 years. I started learning when I was eight and I'm 18 now. We do about 100 hours each year at school, so I have studied for about 1,000 hours in total. I have never been to Britain or the States ...

B Complete each sentence with the correct form of the verb in brackets.

I _____ (work) in this bank for three years. I _____ (start) working here in 2000 and it's 2003 now. I _____ (work) for another bank for a year after I _____ (leave) school, so I _____ (have) two jobs in total. I _____ (visit) several cities in my own country for the bank, but I _____ never _____ (be) abroad.

C Look back at the assignment in Lesson 3 and the notes that you made in Exercise C. Write a first draft of an answer to the assignment. Follow the points in the Skills Check Reminder.

D Exchange your draft with a partner. Discuss points in your partner's draft.

E Write a second draft. Give it to your instructor / teacher.

Task 2: For deductive learners
Read these grammar rules.

The present perfect
There are two forms of this tense:
The simple form: *I have worked.*
We use the simple form in many situations, including:
1 to talk about quantity:
   Example: *I have worked in three different banks.*
2 to talk about experiences:
   Example: *I have been to Britain.*

The continuous form: *I have been working.*
We use the continuous form in several situations, including to talk about length of time.
Example: *I have been living here for five years.*

Skills Check

Reminder
When you write a text, you must ...
- write an introduction.
- write topic sentences to summarise.
- write related paragraphs.
- link sentences.
- use pronouns.

Sometimes you must ...
- give an opinion.
- state reasons.
- compare things.

In this theme you are going to write about the factors that have made you ... you.

Lesson 1: Vocabulary

You are going to learn some of the vocabulary you will need to write about the factors that have influenced your appearance, personality and likes and dislikes.

A Discuss this question. It uses the red words.
What *decisions* should a *parent* make for a *teenager*, and what *decisions* should a *teenager* make for himself or herself?

B Here is your assignment for this theme. Complete the assignment with a green word in each space. Make any necessary changes.

Assignment

What _____ made you the person you are – the way you look, the way you behave, the things you like and dislike?
1. Do some research into the _____ of:
    1.1. _____ – the things a person inherits from parents.
    1.2. _____ – where or how a person is brought up.
2. Make notes of your findings.
3. Write four paragraphs:
    3.1. Para 1: Briefly describe the _____.
    3.2. Paras 2 – 4: Talk about the way heredity and environment _____ your _____, _____ and likes and dislikes.
4. Add an introduction.
5. Add a conclusion.

Vocabulary:

adult *(n)*

decision *(n)*

parent *(n)*

teenager *(n)*

affect *(v)*

appearance *(n)*

effect *(n)*

environment *(n)*

factor *(n)*

heredity *(n)*

personality *(n)*

theory *(n)*

C Make some notes for the second part of the assignment.
1. **1** Complete Table 1 with information about your appearance. Give details of each item and then say who you most resemble in this respect in your family.
2. **2** Complete Table 2 with information about your personality. Which personality trait correctly describes you? Do you think this personality trait comes from a person in your family, or from an experience in your life?
3. **3** Complete Table 3 with your main likes and dislikes. Do you know where your liking or disliking came from – a person or an experience?

Table 1: Appearance

Features	Details	Resemble/s?
eyes		
hair		
height		

Table 2: Personality traits

Traits	Me	From person or experience?
extrovert or introvert?		
optimist or pessimist?		

Table 3: Main likes and dislikes

	Items	From person or experience?
✓✓✓		
✗✗✗		

Lesson 2: Writing

A The writer of this paragraph about appearance has omitted six words.

1 What are the missing words? Where do they go?
2 Write the paragraph again, including the missing words.

> With regard my appearance, I inherited lot of my physical features from parents. My hair and my eyes the same colour as my father's, but I short, like my mother. So I think that I resemble my parents a large extent.

B The writer of this paragraph about personality can't decide between the present simple and the past simple. Choose the correct form of the blue words in each case.

> I think my personality **comes / came** partly from heredity and partly from environment. Firstly, there **is / was** the inherited part. I **am / was** an introvert and I **believe / believed** that I **inherit / inherited** that from my mother. Secondly, there **is / was** the part that **comes / came** from environment. I used to be a pessimist. I **don't / didn't** think anything **can / could** turn out well. Then a teacher **helps / helped** me to get better marks in a maths exam. I **start / started** to try harder and I **am / was** quite optimistic about the future now. So I **think / thought** my environment **changes / changed** my personality in that case.

C The writer of this paragraph about likes can't decide on the correct order for the sentences. Number the sentences in a logical order to make a good paragraph.

___ He played football and tennis with me in the garden from a very early age.
___ However, I don't think this came to me through heredity.
___ My grandfather taught me to love sports.
___ I think that I got this love from my grandfather.
___ As far as my likes are concerned, I love sports.
___ So I don't think that my love of sports is inherited.
___ When I was 10, he started taking me to football matches and tennis games.

D Write three paragraphs about yourself. Use the notes you made in Lesson 1.

Lesson 3: Learning new skills

A You must do research into the effects of heredity (H) and environment (E).

1 Read the article opposite. Use Table 4 to record what each person thought. Write *H* or *E*. Write *?* if there is no information.
2 Add your own opinion.

B How should you finish an opinion paragraph and an opinion essay?

1 Read the final sentence of each paragraph in Lesson 2 Exercises A, B and C. What is each sentence doing?
2 Read the final paragraph of the text opposite. What is it doing?
3 Read the Skills Check and check.

C Write a conclusion:

1 for each of your paragraphs (Lesson 2).
2 to follow the three paragraphs.

Table 4: Theories about heredity and environment

	Appearance	Personality	Likes, etc.
Ancient Romans	H	H	?
Locke			
Mendel			
Watson			
Bouchard			
writer			
me			

Skills Check

Concluding opinions

When you have finished a **paragraph with an opinion**, write a final sentence, summing up. When you have finished an **essay with an opinion**, write a final paragraph, summing up. These conclusions help a reader to understand your opinion.

Example: I believe that my appearance ...

What Makes You ... You?

The effects of heredity and environment

For thousands of years, people have argued about the effects of heredity and environment on the development of children.

Everyone can see that children resemble their parents in appearance, and often in personality, too. The Romans 2,000 years ago had a saying, 'Like father, like son.' However, some philosophers thought these resemblances happened because parents and children lived in the same environment. For example, John Locke, a British philosopher of the 17th century, thought that a baby is like a clean piece of paper – you can write anything on it.

In the 19th century, an Austrian monk called Gregor Mendel did some experiments. He wanted to prove that environment affected physical appearance. He planted two varieties of the same flower next to each other. He then collected and planted seeds from each flower. He was surprised to find that there was no mixing of characteristics in the new plants. He concluded that physical appearance is inherited in plants and in people.

Mendel spent the rest of his life studying plants. He discovered that each living thing inherits one set of characteristics, or genes, from its mother and one from its father. Some characteristics are dominant, which means they take control. In certain circumstances, however, characteristics that are not dominant can appear. This explains why, for example, a child can look more like his grandfather than his father or his brothers.

Inheriting physical characteristics

Imagine that a father and mother both have brown eyes. Brown is a dominant gene (B), but both parents also carry the gene for blue eyes (b) (see Table 5).

These parents have four children. Three have brown eyes, one has blue eyes. Why? Because three of the children inherit at least one dominant gene. Only the fourth child inherits two genes for blue eyes.

Table 5: Inheriting brown or blue eyes

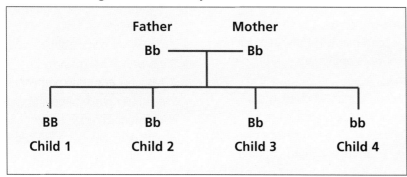

Mendel's work was lost, but it was rediscovered at the start of the 20th century. Inheritance of physical appearance became accepted. Some people, however, continued to believe that environment was more important in deciding personality and likes and dislikes.

In the 1920s, the American psychologist, John B. Watson, argued that environment determines intelligence and character. 'Give me complete control over the environment,' he said, 'and I can make a child into a doctor, lawyer, artist, beggar man or even a thief.'

Many people doubt Watson's ideas that the effect of the environment is so strong. In 1980, another American psychologist, Thomas Bouchard, did some work that threw doubt on the idea of environment having any effect at all. He traced identical twins who were separated at birth. Obviously, these twins were the same in appearance, but he found remarkable similarities in personality and likes and dislikes, as well, even though the children were brought up in completely different environments.

To sum up, it seems that both heredity and environment have an effect on appearance, personality, likes and dislikes.

Lesson 4: Applying new skills

Ⓐ Say that again!

It is often important to be able to say the same thing in a different way, to keep the interest of the reader. Find another way (on the right) to say each thing on the left.

1	as far as appearance is concerned	**a**	How does heredity affect a child?
2	my appearance	**b**	I am an introverted person.
3	my personality	**c**	I inherited my eyes from my father.
4	I am an introvert.	**d**	It comes from where and how you were brought up.
5	My eyes come from my father.	**e**	My mother is short and so am I.
6	I am short, like my mother.	**f**	the way I behave
7	It comes from your environment.	**g**	the way I look
8	What is the effect of heredity on a child?	**h**	with regard to appearance

Ⓑ For the assignment (Lesson 1) you need to describe briefly theories about heredity and environment.

1 Read the Skills Check.

2 Look at Table 6 below. The information is correct but mixed up. Make a new table with the correct names, dates, nationalities and beliefs / findings.

3 Read the article from Lesson 3 again and check.

Ⓒ Look again at Table 4 (Lesson 2) and Table 6 (below). Complete each of these sentences with something suitable. Don't look at the article itself.

1 John Locke, a British _____ of the 17th century, _____ that a baby is like a clean sheet of paper. He _____ that environment affects personality.

2 In the _____ century, an Austrian _____ called Gregor Mendel _____ that appearance in plants is inherited. He _____ that heredity produces appearance in people.

3 John B. Watson was an American _____. He _____, in the 1920s, that he could make a child into a doctor, lawyer, artist, beggar man or even a thief. He _____, like Locke, that environment produces personality.

4 An _____ psychologist, Thomas Bouchard, studied identical twins in _____. He _____ that personality and likes and dislikes can be inherited, as well as appearance.

> ### Skills Check
>
> Talking about famous people
>
> When we write about a famous person in history, we usually tell the reader:
>
> **1** his or her **dates** or when he / she lived, e.g., *17th century; the 1920s.*
>
> **2** his or her **nationality**.
>
> **3** his or her **profession**.
>
> **4** his or her **invention** or **theory***. We usually name people in chronological order, so the reader does not get confused about the order of events.
>
> *We can use the present tense for a theory.*

Ⓓ Write a paragraph, briefly describing the theories about heredity and environment.

Ⓔ Write an introduction to your essay, explaining what you are going to write about.

Table 6: Key figures in the heredity / environment debate

Name	Nationality	Profession	Date	Belief / Findings
Gregor Mendel	American	monk	17th C	'a baby is like a clean piece of paper'
John B. Watson	American	philosopher	19th C	'can make a child into a doctor, lawyer, artist, beggar man or even a thief'
John Locke	Austrian	psychologist	1920s	appearance is inherited in plants and people
Thomas Bouchard	British	psychologist	1980	personality, likes and dislikes can be inherited, as well as appearance

In this theme you are going to write about recruiting and dismissing people.

Lesson 1: Vocabulary

You are going to learn some of the vocabulary you will need to write the texts.

A Write one sentence with each of the eight red words.

B Complete the text with a green word in each space. Make any necessary changes.

Flow charts are a way of showing the stages of a process. For example, Figure 1 shows a very simple _____ process. In other words, it shows the way that a company gets a new employee. Flow charts are very useful when several people are involved in the _____. Here are the basic principles to follow when you draw a flow chart:

1. All the processes must come between the START point and the END point. We write these points in rectangles with rounded corners.

2. Flow charts contain ACTIONS and DECISIONS.
    2.1. _____ are things we do in the process. We write them in rectangular boxes. We usually write in the imperative, e.g., _____ *for new person*. There is one entry point and one exit point from an action box.
    2.2. _____ are things we have to think about. We write them in diamond-shaped boxes. We must write decisions as Yes/No questions. We often just write one or two words, e.g., _____? = *Does the person have suitable qualifications, like a degree or a college certificate?* _____ = *Has the person worked in this kind of job before?* _____? = *Does the person's employer or college lecturer think they would be good for this job?* There is one entry point and two exit points from a decision box. The exit points are YES and NO.

3. The normal flow through the process is down. However, lines with arrowheads show other directions at times.

C Study the flow chart in Figure 1. What do these green words mean?
   1 appoint
   2 reject

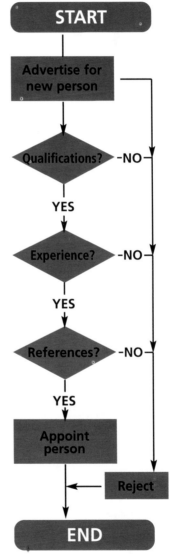

Figure 1: A recruitment process

administrator *(n)*
conclude *(v)*
equipment *(n)*
furniture *(n)*
purchase *(v)*
recommendation *(n)*
report *(n)*
resource *(n)*
action *(n)*
advertise *(v)*
appoint *(v)*
decision *(n)*
experience *(n)*
process *(n)*
qualification *(n)*
recruitment *(n)*
reference *(n)*
reject *(v)*

Lesson 2: Writing

A The words in the box are formal verbs used to talk about recruitment.

> apply for   appoint   draw up   evaluate   insert   interview   produce   receive

1 Write a formal verb from the box after each informal verb in the left-hand column below. Check with a dictionary.

Example: give the job to = *appoint*

2 Match the verbs with the nouns / phrases to make the stages of a recruitment process. Copy each phrase onto a separate card.

Example: *appoint the best applicant*

a	give the job to	_*appoint*_	**1**	a job description
b	check	_____	**2**	a short list of applicants
c	talk to	_____	**3**	an advertisement in the local newspaper
d	make	_____	**4**	applicants
e	put	_____	**5**	applications
f	get	_____	**6**	references
g	send for	_____	**7**	the applications
h	write	_____	**8**	the best applicant
i	choose	_____	**9**	the applicant for a trial period

B Put the stages in Exercise A in a logical order. Give reasons for the order.

C Describe the process as the manager of the company. Use *We* ….

Remember!

- Group stages of the process into two or three paragraphs.
- Write topic sentences.
- Join short sentences with *and*.

- Add reasons for some of the stages with *because, so, therefore*.
- Use sequencers – *Firstly, Secondly, Next, After that, Then, Finally*.

Lesson 3: Learning new skills

A As we learnt in Lesson 1, we can show a process as a flow chart.

1 Complete Figure 2 with a suitable word in each space.

2 Explain the recruitment process in this flow chart.

B Read your process again from Lesson 2. Does the flow chart in Figure 2 accurately show *your* process?

C In Lesson 2, you wrote as the manager of the company with *We* …

1 Read the Skills Check.

2 Find and underline each verb in your text from Lesson 2. Work out the passive form.

D Write about your process again, using the passive.

Skills Check

Writing about processes

We often use the **passive form** when we write about a process.

Examples:

active	passive
*We **receive** applications.*	*Applications **are received**.*

Notes:

1 There is no person – *I* , *we, he* – in passive sentences. In a process, we are not interested in the person.

2 We make the passive with a form of *be* + the past participle.

Example: *are received*

3 The past participle of regular verbs is the same as the past tense. Most formal verbs are regular.

Example: *receive – received*

4 You must learn the past participle of irregular verbs.

Example: *draw – drawn*

Figure 2: A selection procedure flow chart

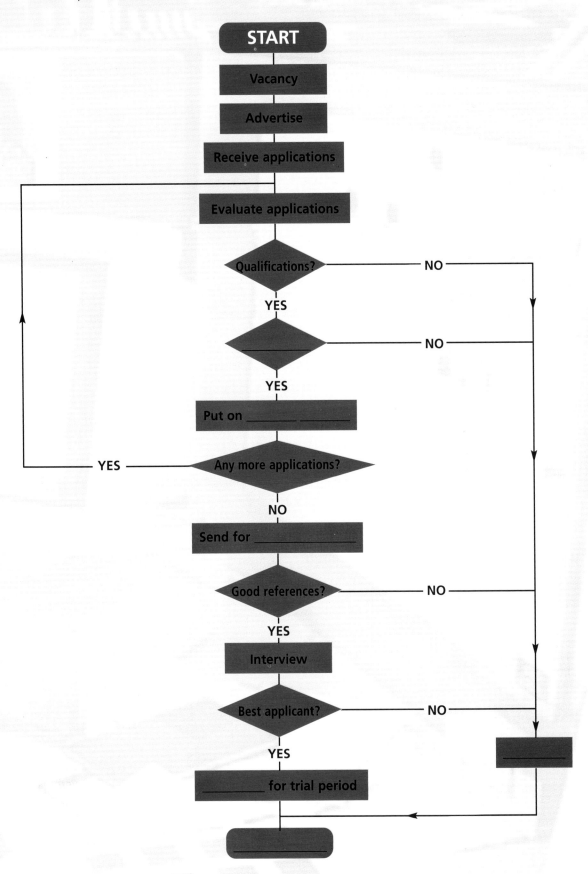

Lesson 4: Applying new skills

A In a recruitment process, what can you ...

insert? draw up? appoint? receive?

apply for? interview? evaluate? reject?

B Imagine you decide to advertise all jobs *inside* your company first, and only advertise in the newspaper if there are no suitable people. What changes must you make to the flow chart in Figure 2 on page 17?

C You are going to write about another process.

1 Look at Figure 3. Can you guess the meaning of *disciplinary*?

2 What happens in this process ...

   a when a complaint is received?

   b if this is the first complaint?

   c if this is the second complaint?

   d if this is the third complaint?

   e if this is the fourth complaint?

D Think about the disciplinary process in your university or college.

1 Write each stage on a separate card.

2 Put the cards in a logical order.

3 Draw the process as a flow chart.

E Write a description of the disciplinary process in your university or college.

Remember:

- Use the passive.
- Join short sentences with *and*.
- Give reasons for parts of the process with *because, so, therefore*.
- If it is a long process, divide the information into paragraphs and write a topic sentence for each paragraph.

Figure 3: Flow chart for disciplinary procedure

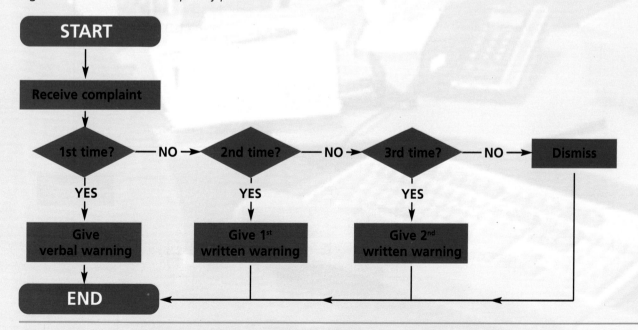

In this theme you are going to describe how to cool a room efficiently.

Lesson 1: Vocabulary

You are going to learn some vocabulary that you need to write the report.

A Think about an engineering *project* in your area.
1 What is the *aim* of the project?
2 What are they *constructing*?
3 What have they *achieved* so far?
4 Do you know any of the *facts and figures* about the project?

B Read the text. Look at Figure 1. Complete the text with a green word in each space. Make any necessary changes.

Figure 1: Energy use in the home

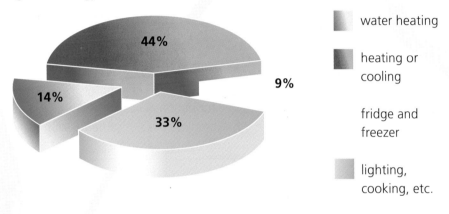

- water heating
- heating or cooling
- fridge and freezer
- lighting, cooking, etc.

What uses the most _____ in your home? Is it the water heating? What about the lighting system? How about cooking, or the fridge and freezer?

In fact, it is none of these. You use the most energy to _____ your house with radiators or _____ your house with air conditioners. Scientists _____ that heating or cooling typically comprises 44% of household energy use (see Figure 1), so you will save a lot of money if do not _____ energy on heating or cooling.

Unfortunately, we do waste a lot of energy, however. Houses in cold climates _____ a lot of energy because they are not _____ properly. Similarly, houses in hot climates don't have _____ on the roof or windows, so they _____ a lot of heat from the sun.

C Discuss these questions.
1 How many radiators do you have in your house? What about air conditioners?
2 Is your house insulated?
3 Do you think you waste energy at home? How?

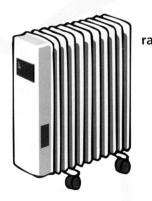

radiator

air conditioner

achieve *(v)*

aim *(n)*

construct *(v)*

facts and figures *(n)*

fresh (water) *(adj)*

project *(n)*

structure *(n)*

calculate *(v)*

cool *(v)*

energy *(n)*

gain *(v)*

heat *(v)*

insulate *(v)*

insulated *(adj)*

insulation *(n)*

lose *(v)*

waste *(v)*

Lesson 2: Writing

A Imagine you live in a cold country. Which room(s) in your house would need the most heating?
   1 Write the main rooms in order. Explain your order.
   2 Look at Figure 1 opposite and check your answers.

B How does heat escape from a house?
   1 Discuss in pairs.
   2 Look at Figure 2 opposite and check your ideas.

C How can you stop heat escaping?
   1 Discuss in pairs.
   2 Look at Table 1 opposite and check your ideas.

D Look at the essay on the opposite page. Work through the activities in the green box.

E Cover the text. How much can you remember from the illustrations?

para	activities
1	Write the correct verb in each space.
2	**a** Write a noun in each space.
	b Write a new final sentence for a room with different dimensions.
3	**a** Write a preposition / particle in each space.
	b Write one more sentence about a *living room*.
4	**a** Look at Figure 2. Write the correct information in each space.
	b Complete the last sentence with something suitable.
5	**a** Why does the writer change from *can* in the first sentence to *could* in the second sentence?
	b Can you guess the meaning of *thermostat* and *boiler*?
6	**a** Look at Table 1. Write the correct information in each space.
	b Complete the last sentence with something suitable.

Lesson 3: Learning new skills

A Imagine you live in a cold country. Think about the room that you are in.
   1 What is the volume?
   2 What size radiator would you need?
   3 How could you improve the insulation?

B Look at the text opposite.
   1 Find and copy the topic sentences.
   Example:
   Para 1: *Imagine that you have decided to install a radiator in a room for the first time.*
   2 Cover the text. What information do you expect to find after each topic sentence?
   3 Write one more piece of information after each topic sentence.
   4 Uncover the text and check your ideas.

C Read the Skills Check.
   1 Find each example sentence in the text opposite and complete it.
   2 Write one more sentence with each pattern.

D Test each other in pairs on the spelling of new words from Lesson 2.

Joining sentences (1)

You can join two sentences to show different relationships.
Examples:

reason	*You can heat a kitchen less than other rooms*	**because** *there will often be …*
consequence	*Bathrooms need the most heating*	**so** *a bathroom of the same size ….*
condition	*The radiator should be adequate to heat the room*	**if** *you calculate …*
purpose	*You must calculate the volume of the room*	*(if you want)* **to** *discover …*

Note:
With **reason**, **condition** and **purpose** sentences, you can change the order of the two halves.

Figure 1: Radiator requirements for various room sizes   Figure 2: Heat loss from the average house

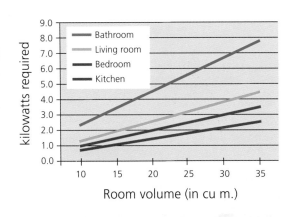

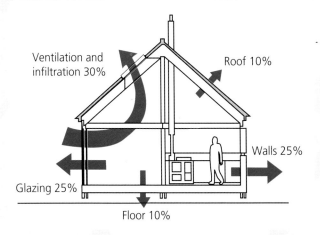

Table 1: Solutions to heat loss

Area	Solution	Cost
floor	lay carpet	$$
roof	insulate the roof or the loft	$$
walls	put in cavity wall insulation	$$$
	put insulation on the outside wall	$
windows	install double-glazed windows	$$$
draughts	find and stop cold draughts round windows and under doors	$

① Imagine that you have _____ to install a radiator in a room for the first time. Perhaps you _____ a coal or wood fire in the room before. It is very important to _____ the right size of radiator. The correct radiator will _____ the room comfortably in winter.

② To discover the correct _____ of radiator for a particular room, you must calculate the volume of the _____. The formula for the _____ of a cube is length times width times _____. For example, if the room is 3 metres by 4 metres by 2.5 _____, the volume is 3 x 4 x 2.5 = 30 cubic metres (m³).

③ You must then consider which room the radiator is _____. Generally speaking, you can heat a kitchen less _____ other rooms because there will often be extra heat _____ cooking. For example, a kitchen _____ 30 m³ needs a radiator that produces one kilowatt (kW) _____ heat per hour (see Figure 1). Bathrooms, _____ the other hand, need the most heating, so a bathroom _____ the same size needs a radiator _____ an output of 2 kW.

④ If you calculate the volume of the room correctly, the radiator should be adequate to heat the room to a comfortable temperature, even in winter. However, on average, a room loses _____ of its heat through the walls, another 25% through the _____ and a further 10% each through the floor and _____. The final 30% is lost through _____. If the correct size of radiator does not heat the room properly, _____.

⑤ What can you do? You could increase the size of the radiator or turn up the thermostat on the boiler. However, these are not energy-efficient solutions. It is much better to improve the insulation of the room.

⑥ Some improvements in insulation do not cost very much money, while others are expensive. For example, you can lay a cheap _____ to reduce the heat loss through the floor. You can also find and fill gaps around and under doors and around windows to stop _____. Insulating the loft is not very expensive, either. Other improvements are quite expensive. For example, it will cost a lot of money to put in cavity wall insulation or install double-glazed _____. However, you will _____.

Lesson 4: Applying new skills

Ⓐ Copy and complete these sentences. Refer to the illustrations (Lesson 3) but don't look at the text.

1 It is very important to …

2 The correct radiator will …

3 To discover the correct size of radiator for a particular room, you must …

4 For example, if the room is 3 metres by 4 metres by 2.5 metres, the volume …

5 You must then consider which …

6 Generally speaking, you can heat a kitchen less than other rooms because …

7 For example, a kitchen of 30 m³ needs a radiator that …

8 If you calculate the volume of the room correctly, the radiator …

9 However, on average, a room loses …

10 If the correct size of radiator does not heat the room properly, you …

11 What can you do? You could …

12 It is much better to …

13 Some improvements in insulation do not …

14 For example, you can …

15 Other improvements are quite expensive. For example, it will cost a lot of money …

Ⓑ Look at Figure 1. What size a/c do you need to cool the room that you are in?

Ⓒ You are going to write about cooling a room.

1 Look at the figure and tables below. Ask about words you don't understand.

2 Plan your writing (see the Skills Check).

3 Do a first draft. Use sentence patterns from Lesson 3.

4 Exchange drafts with a partner.

5 Write a final version.

Figure 1: A/C requirements for various room sizes

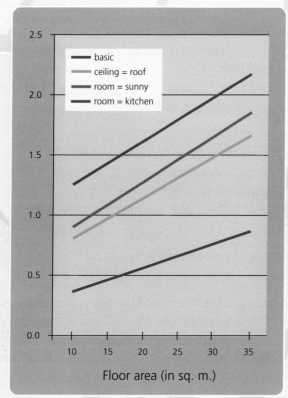

Floor area (in sq. m.)

legend:
- basic
- ceiling = roof
- room = sunny
- room = kitchen

Table 1: Energy-saving tips

Area	Solution	Cost
draughts	find and stop warm draughts around windows, wall a/cs and under doors	$
room	install a fan to spread the cooled air more efficiently	$$
outside	plant shrubs to shade the a/c compressor unit	$$
	install awnings outside windows	$$
roof	insulate with a highly reflective material	$$$
windows	close curtains during the day	$
	put up white window blinds to reflect the heat away	$$
	glaze with energy-efficient glass (see Table 2)	$$$

Table 2: Heat gain for glazing types

Glazing types	% heat gain
single-glazed, clear	79%
double-glazed, clear	58%
double-glazed, bronze	48%
single-glazed, spectrally selective	31%
double-glazed, spectrally selective	26%

In this theme you are going to write about an extraction industry in your area.

Lesson 1: Vocabulary

You are going to learn some vocabulary you need to talk about extraction industries.

A Look at the table and the map. Write a red word in each space in the table.
Label the map with information from the table.

Table 1: South Africa

_____	At the southern tip of the _____ of Africa
_____	Mostly desert, but subtropical along the east coast; sunny days, cool nights
_____	1,219,912 sq km
_____	44 m
_____	Namibia, Botswana and Zimbabwe in the north. Mozambique and Swaziland in the east. Lesotho is completely surrounded by S. A.
_____	Gold is the _____ product. It is produced in the region around Johannesburg.
_____	Corn is grown in the northeast, wheat in the northeast and southwest and sugarcane on the east coast.

Figure 1: South Africa

agriculture *(n)*

area *(n)*

border *(n)*

climate *(n)*

continent *(n)*

industry *(n)*

location *(n)*

main *(adj)*

population *(n)*

extraction *(n)*

fossil fuel *(n)*

metal *(n)*

mine *(v)*

mining *(n)*

petroleum *(n)*

producer *(n)*

product *(n)*

B Cover the table. Talk about the country using the information on the map.

C In Lesson 2 you are going to read more about gold. Complete the text with a green word in each space.

South Africa is an important _____ of gold (Au) and iron (Fe). These _____ are taken from the ground through _____, which usually involves digging a deep hole in the ground. South Africa makes many _____ from the metals, including jewellery from gold and steel from iron. The country also produces _____, including _____, which is used to power cars and to make electricity. South Africa also _____ diamonds and other precious stones. Taking metals, fossil fuels or precious stones from the ground is called _____.

D Work in groups. Answer the questions.
1 Can you think of any other words in English for …
     metals?   fossil fuels?   precious stones?
2 What else can you make from …
     gold?   petroleum?
3 Mining 'usually involves digging a deep hole'. How else can you mine for things?
4 What extraction industries do you have in your country?

Lesson 2: Writing

A Imagine you have to write about gold mining. What topics could you include?

B Read the topic sentences in the green box from an essay about gold. They form a summary of the essay.
1 Complete the topic sentences with a noun from the yellow box. Make any necessary changes.
2 What information do you expect to find in the rest of each paragraph?
3 Check your answers to 1 and 2 with the text opposite.

C Look at the second sentence in the first paragraph of the text opposite.
1 What form is *believe* in?
2 What about *produce*?

D Look at Paragraphs 1 to 4. There are some mistakes with the verbs. Cross out *was* or *were* in eight places.

E Look at Paragraph 5. Write *is* or *are* in front of each past participle to make the correct passive form.

F Read Paragraphs 6 to 10. Write a linking word in each space.

Lesson 3: Learning new skills

A Read each topic sentence in Lesson 2 Exercise B again. What information appeared in each paragraph?

B Paragraphs 2 and 5 describe processes.
1 Illustrate each process.
2 Cover the text. Write one paragraph about each process.

C How can you continue each sentence in the blue box?
1 Read the Skills Check.
2 Think of a possible ending, then check with the text opposite.
3 Cover the text and complete each sentence with something suitable.

> **a** The ancient Egyptians had gold mines, which ...
> **b** The water is passed through a sieve, which ...
> **c** Gold is also used to make a wide range of products, which ...
> **d** South Africa has reserves of approximately 36 million kilos, which ...
> **e** The main gold-mining area of South Africa is the Witwatersrand region, which ...
> **f** Most of the gold is extracted from underground mines, which ...

---

1 In ancient times, there were many _____ about the origins of gold.

2 In fact, gold is formed in the _____ of the Earth.

3 Gold was probably the first _____ that people discovered.

4 In 1848, a small _____ of gold was discovered by John Sutter in California.

5 There are three _____ of extracting gold.

6 Gold has many special _____.

7 We can make a large number of _____ from gold.

8 The main _____ of gold in the world is South Africa.

9 The main gold-mining _____ of South Africa is the Witwatersrand region.

10 The future for South African _____ does not look good.

---

area   centre   gold mining   metal
producer   product   property
quantity   theory   way

Skills Check

Joining sentences (2)

You can sometimes join two sentences with **which**. You can do this if the **object** of Sentence 1 is the **subject** of Sentence 2.
Examples:

Sentence 1		Sentence 2
The country produces around 350,000 kilos per annum.	, which	~~350,000 kilos per annum~~ is just over a third of world production of gold.

Note: Change the **full stop** at the end of Sentence 1 to a **comma** and delete the **subject** of Sentence 2.

1   In ancient times, there were many theories about the origins of gold. People in some countries believed that gold was produced by volcanoes. Other people thought that it grew from a certain kind of earth. Some were said it was created by lightning, while others were believed that at one time it was rained gold.

2   In fact, gold was formed in the centre of the Earth. It was flowed up like a river and formed 'veins' or lines within rock. In some places, the rock was eroded by rain and wind, and the gold was washed into streams.

3   Gold was probably the first metal that people were discovered. People found small pieces of gold in river beds. They were made the gold into jewellery and coins. The earliest gold jewellery dates from about 3000 BCE. It was found by archaeologists in the area between the Tigris and Euphrates rivers in southern Iraq. We know that the ancient Egyptians had gold mines, which were probably at Wadi Hammamat near Naqada. Gold was also mined for thousands of years in India, Turkey and China.

4   In 1848, a small quantity of gold was discovered by John Sutter in California. This discovery was led to a 'gold rush'. Thousands of people left their jobs and their homes. They were travelled to the area to make their fortunes. There were similar gold rushes after discoveries in Australia in 1851, and in other parts of the United States, including Alaska, in 1899.

5   There are three ways of extracting gold. They _____ called panning, surface mining and underground mining. In panning, rivers with particles of gold _____ diverted through a number of lakes. After each lake, the water _____ passed through a sieve, which catches the particles of gold. In ancient times, the coat of a sheep was used instead of a sieve. In surface mining, the rock and earth above a vein of gold _____ dug away and the gold vein _____ uncovered. In underground mining, vertical shafts _____ dug down into a vein of gold. Then horizontal shafts __ dug to follow the vein.

6   Gold has many special properties. It is beautiful to look at _____ easy to work with. You can pull it into very long wires. You can _____ beat it into very thin sheets. Gold does not rust or lose its colour, _____ it is very long-lasting. It is _____ a very good conductor of heat and electricity.

7   We can make a large number of products from gold. The main product is still jewellery, _____ gold is flexible and beautiful. Gold is _____ used to make a wide range of products, _____ include teeth and parts of electronic devices. For example, the battery connectors on your mobile phone are probably made of gold. Gold lasts a long time, _____ it is also used to make coins and medals.

8   The main producer of gold in the world is South Africa. The country produces around 350,000 kilos per annum, _____ is just over a third of world production of gold. South Africa has reserves of approximately 36 million kilos, _____ is around 40% of world reserves.

9   The main gold-mining area of South Africa is the Witwatersrand region, _____ was the site of the first discovery of gold in the country in 1884. A gold rush started, _____ Johannesburg was founded in Witwatersrand in 1886 as a gold-mining town.

10   The future for South African gold mining does not look good. Most of the gold is extracted from underground mines, _____ are up to 3.8 kilometres deep, _____ production costs are high. For example, it costs $7.83 to extract one gram of South African gold, _____ it only costs $5.96 for one gram of Canadian gold.

Lesson 4: Applying new skills

Ⓐ What are the missing words in each of these sentences from the text in Lessons 2 and 3?

1 People in some countries believed that gold _____ produced by volcanoes.
2 Gold flowed up _____ a river and formed 'veins' or lines _____ rock.
3 The earliest gold jewellery _____ from about 3000 BCE.
4 Thousands of people left _____ jobs and _____ homes.
5 In surface mining, the rock and earth above a vein of gold _____ dug away and the gold vein _____ uncovered.
6 Gold does not rust or lose _____ colour, _____ it is very long-lasting.
7 Gold is _____ used to make a wide range of products, which _____ teeth and parts of electronic devices.
8 South Africa _____ around 350,000 kilos per annum, _____ is just over a third of world production of gold.
9 A gold rush started, and Johannesburg was _____ in Witwatersrand in 1886 as a gold-mining town.
10 Most of _____ gold is extracted from underground mines, which _____ up to 3.8 kilometres deep, _____ production costs are high.

Ⓑ What is the noun from each of these verbs?

verb	noun
discover	
form	
mine	
produce	
extract	

Ⓒ You are going to write about an extraction industry in your area. You are going to use the same writing plan as the text in Lessons 2 and 3.

1 Choose the industry – for example, *coal, petroleum, diamonds, silver* ...
2 Study the text about gold on the previous page. Make a writing plan in your notebook. Leave space for notes (see Figure 1).
3 Work in groups. Choose one or more topics from your writing plan and do research into the topics. Make notes. Tell the other people in your group the information you discovered.

Ⓓ Write your essay.
Remember:

• Write a topic sentence for each paragraph. Together, the topic sentences should form a summary of the essay.
• Develop each paragraph from the topic sentence.
• Join short sentences with *and, because, so, therefore.*
• Add more information about the object in a sentence with *which.*
• Show connections between sentences with *also.*

Figure 1: Writing plan

Paragraph	Notes
1 Early theories of formation	
2 True formation	
3 Early discoveries	
4	

In this theme you are going to write about your own or another civilization.

Lesson 1: Vocabulary

You are going to learn some of the vocabulary you will need for your essay.

A Write one sentence each with five of the red words. Write about your own culture.

B Read the extract from a text about civilizations. Write one of the green words in each space. Make any necessary changes.

C Study a student's spidergram of a civilization. Write long answers to these questions.

1 What is the name? Why does it have that name?
2 What is the number, according to historians?
3 Which civilization is it related to?
4 Where did it start?
5 When did it start?
6 When did it end?

D What do you know about the advances of Islamic civilization?

1 Add examples of each kind of advance.
2 Write one sentence each about the advances you have noted.

According to the British historian, Professor Arnold Toynee, there have been 21 civilizations. Other historians say that the number is 26 or 27. Many civilizations _____ earlier ones. Eight civilizations still _____. In other words, they continue to grow and to make _____ in science, industry and _____ – painting, music, literature. We recognise civilizations by their _____, especially the public buildings, and by the system of _____, i.e., the way the civilization deals with crime.

bride *(n)*

ceremony (ies) *(n)*

engagement *(n)*

groom *(n)*

marriage *(n)*

married *(adj)*

wedding *(n)*

advance *(n)*

architecture *(n)*

flourish *(v)*

law *(n)*

relate (to) *(v)*

the arts *(n)*

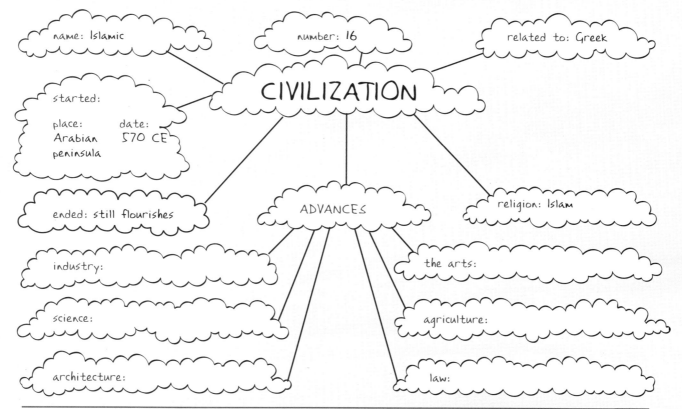

name: Islamic

number: 16

related to: Greek

started:
place: Arabian peninsula   date: 570 CE

CIVILIZATION

ended: still flourishes

ADVANCES

religion: Islam

industry:

the arts:

science:

agriculture:

architecture:

law:

Lesson 2: Writing

A Read the topic sentences in the blue box. They are from the main body of an essay about a civilization.
1 Write a preposition in each space.
2 Make a spidergram of the topic of each paragraph.
3 What information do you expect to find in each paragraph? Add ideas to your spidergram.

B Read the main body of the essay (opposite).
1 Check your answers to Exercise A.
2 Add information from each paragraph to your spidergram.

C Read the main body of the essay again. Write a joining word in each space.

D Cover the essay. Give the main information from each paragraph from your spidergram.

Lesson 3: Learning new skills

A Read the words from Lesson 2 in the green box.
1 Add the correct vowel(s).
2 Write one sentence each with five of the words.

a h__st__r____n	**g** spr____d
b fl____r__sh	**h** __mpr__v__
c d__sc__v__ry	**i** __gr__c__lt__r__
d __nv__nt____n	**j** m__d__c__n__
e __rch__t__ct__r__	**k** kn__wl__dg__
f __dv__nc__	**l** pr__d__ct____n

B Read the first sentence of the essay opposite.
1 Find the second verb. What form is it in? What is the subject?
2 Read the Skills Check and check your answers.
3 Find and underline more participles from the essay. What was the original subject and verb form?

C Rewrite each sentence with a participle as two sentences.

D Cover the text. Join the sentences again with the correct participle.

- Western civilization is related _____ the Greek and Roman civilizations, which flourished _____ about 1300 BCE to _____ 100 CE.
- Western civilization began _____ about 675 CE _____ Ireland, _____ the western edge ___ Europe.
- _____ the early centuries _____ Western civilization, there were very few important inventions or discoveries, because the civilization was coming _____ of 'The Dark Ages'.
- The first major advance _____ Western civilization was made _____ Johannes Gutenberg.
- The arts flourished _____ the period _____ about 1485 _____ about 1650, called 'The Renaissance', or rebirth.
- Industry made huge advances _____ the period called the Industrial Revolution, which started _____ the end _____ the 17th century.
- There are many other things that we think _____ as Western.

1 According to some historians, there have been 26 or 27 civilizations, beginning with the Egyptian civilization over 6,000 years ago. Eight of these civilizations still flourish, including Western civilization and Islamic civilization. In this essay, I describe the growth of Western civilization and give examples of some of its advances.

2 Western civilization is related to the Greek and Roman civilizations, _____ flourished from about 1300 BCE to around 100 CE. However, the civilization did not develop directly from those earlier civilizations, _____ most of the important advances of the Greeks and the Romans were lost for hundreds of years. They were finally rediscovered by Arabs, who translated a lot of ancient learning, exporting it later to the West.

3 Western civilization began in about 675 CE in Ireland, at the western edge of Europe. Monks moved to Wales and Scotland on the mainland of Britain _____, from there, the Christian civilization moved eastwards over several centuries, spreading to Scandinavia, France, Germany, Italy and northern Spain.

4 In the early centuries of Western civilization, there were very few important inventions or discoveries, _____ the civilization was coming out of 'The Dark Ages'. This name refers to the period of poor knowledge _____ lasted from about 500 CE to about 1000 CE. There was very little education of young people _____ there were very few schools or universities.

5  The first major advance of Western civilization was made by Johannes Gutenberg. He was a German printer who lived from about 1397 to 1468 CE. In around 1450 CE, he invented a machine _____ speed up the production of printed books. The new cheap books _____ the machine produced spread the knowledge of earlier civilizations, translated in many cases by Arab scholars of Greek and Latin.

6 The arts flourished in the period from about 1485 to about 1650, called 'The Renaissance', or rebirth. During this period, for example, Leonardo da Vinci produced his paintings and Shakespeare wrote his plays.

7 Industry made huge advances in the period called the Industrial Revolution, _____ started at the end of the 17th Century. Thomas Savery was a British engineer who invented a simple steam engine in 1698 _____ pump water out of a flooded mine. Thomas Newcomen, a British blacksmith, improved Savery's engine _____, for the first time, steam power was used in industry. The invention of the steam engine led to the production of steam trains, _____ metal ships powered by steam. In 1886, Karl Benz, a German engineer, obtained a patent for a motor car, _____ led directly to the modern world of transport, including air travel.

8 There are many other things that we think of as Western. For example, in architecture, there is the skyscraper. In science, work on recording and reproducing sound formed the basis of the modern telecommunications industry, _____ work on recording and reproducing moving pictures led to the development of television and the movie industry. In agriculture, plant diseases are now controlled by pesticides, _____ in medicine, human diseases are controlled by drugs. Above all, Western civilization has taken the Greek idea of democracy as the basis for all government.

9 To sum up, Western civilization has a large number of impressive advances to its name. There does not seem any end to the civilization at the moment.

Lesson 4: Applying new skills

A Read the first two paragraphs of the essay from Lesson 2 again.
 1 Think of a verb for each space. Decide if it should be active, passive or a participle.
 2 Check with the text on page 29.

According to some historians, there _____ 26 or 27 civilizations, _____ with the Egyptian civilization over 6,000 years ago. Eight of these civilizations still _____, _____ Western civilization and Islamic civilization. In this essay I _____ the growth of Western civilization and _____ examples of some of its advances.

    Western civilization _____ to the Greek and Roman civilizations, which _____ from about 1300 BCE to around 100 CE. However, the civilization _____ not _____ directly from those earlier civilizations, because most of the important advances of the Greeks and the Romans _____ for hundreds of years. They _____ finally _____ by Arabs, who _____ a lot of ancient learning, _____ it later to the West.

B How can you continue each sentence in the yellow box?
 1 Read the Skills Check.
 2 Think of a possible ending, then check with the text on page 29.
 3 Cover the text and complete each sentence.

> **a** Johannes Gutenberg was a German printer who ...
> **b** Thomas Savery was a British engineer who ...
> **c** Thomas Newcomen was a British blacksmith who ...
> **d** Shakespeare was a playwright who ...
> **e** Leonardo da Vinci was a painter who ...
> **f** Karl Benz was a German engineer who ...

C You are going to write about a civilization that still flourishes – your own or another one. You are going to use the same writing plan as the essay in Lesson 2.
 1 Choose the civilization.
 2 Make a spidergram of topics.
 3 Number the topics in a logical order.
 4 Do some research and add information to your spidergram.
 5 Write your essay.
 6 Write an introduction and a conclusion.

Skills Check

Joining sentences (4)

You can sometimes join two sentences with **who**. You can do this if the subject of the second sentence is a person or people.

Example:

Sentence 1		Sentence 2
They were rediscovered by Arabs.	**who**	~~The Arabs~~ translated a lot of ancient learning.

Note: Delete the **full stop** at the end of Sentence 1 and the **subject** of Sentence 2.

Table 1: Civilizations that flourish

Civilization	Start date
Far Eastern	c. 645 CE
Western	c. 675 CE
Orthodox (Turkey)	c. 680 CE
Hindu	c. 775 CE
Orthodox (Russia)	c. 950 CE
Islamic	570 CE

REMEMBER!

- **Write a topic sentence for each paragraph. Together, the topic sentences should form a summary of the essay.**
- **Develop each paragraph from the topic sentence.**
- **Join short sentences with *and, because, so, therefore, which, who, that.***

_____ _____ _____

_____

_____

decide *(v)*

develop *(v)*

produce *(v)*

reach *(v)*

realise *(v)*

sell *(v)*

solve *(v)*

think (of) *(v)*

work *(v)* (= do the job correctly)

appliance *(n)*

device *(n)*

dishwasher *(n)*

electric iron *(n)*

labour-saving *(adj)*

microwave oven *(n)*

refrigerator *(n)*

vacuum cleaner *(n)*

washing machine *(n)*

In this theme you are going to write about a modern household appliance.

Lesson 1 Vocabulary

Ⓐ What is the verb for each noun in Table 1? Cover the red words, complete the table then check.

Ⓑ There are many appliances in the home that save labour (or work). We call these 'labour-saving devices'. Label the four devices above with a green word or phrase. Which two devices in the word list are not shown? Do you know what they are?

Ⓒ Which device was invented first?
  1 Number the devices in order.
  2 Study Table 2 below. Copy a device into each space.
  3 Check your ideas in C1.

Ⓓ Read about one of the inventions.

Ⓔ Write a paragraph about another invention.

Table 1: Some nouns and verbs

noun	verb
decision	
development	
production	
solution	
sale	
thought	

Food goes bad at room temperature, so in the old days people did not keep food for very long. In 1803, an American engineer, Thomas Moore, solved the problem by inventing the refrigerator. However, the first home refrigerator was not sold until 1911.

Table 2: Problems and solutions in labour-saving in the home

Problem	Original solution	Invention	Inventor	Date	Notes
food goes bad at room temperature	do not keep food for very long		Thomas Moore (US) – engineer	1803	first home refrigerator was not sold until 1911
clothes get dirty when you wear them	hit them with rocks in water		James King (US) – inventor	1851	powered by hand
clothes get creased when you wear them	press with a piece of hot metal		Henry Seeley (US) – inventor	1882	weighed almost seven kilos, took a long time to warm up
dishes get dirty when you use them	wash them up by hand		Josephine Cochran (US) – housewife	1889	powered by hand; said, 'If no one else will invent it, I will.'
floors and carpets get covered in dust and dirt	sweep with a brush; beat carpets with a stick		John Thurman (US) – businessman	1899	powered by petrol
ovens take a long time to cook food	start cooking a long time before the meal is wanted		Dr. Percy Spencer (US) – scientist	1946	chocolate melted in Spencer's pocket when he was near a microwave machine

Lesson 2: Writing

A Which labour-saving device saves the most work, in your opinion?

B Read the first five paragraphs of an essay
(opposite) about a labour-saving device.
   1 Copy each clause in the blue box into the
   correct place in the text (a to h).
   2 Write **one word** in each of the other spaces.

C Read Paragraph 5 again. Decide which participle
(in italics) is correct in each case.

- began to change all that
- did heavy manual work
- was an American inventor
- was a flat piece of wood with bumps in it
- was required
- was called the *Thor*
- were extremely muddy or dusty
- were full of smoke

D Read Paragraph 6.
   1 Decide if part of the verb *be* is required in each space, to make the sentence passive.
   2 If it is required, write the correct form – *is* or *are*.

E Read the whole essay again. Write a good concluding paragraph.

Lesson 3: Learning new skills

A Make a sentence from the essay opposite with
each verb / verb phrase in the yellow box.

save	improve
do by hand	spin
reduce	pump
power	programme

B The essay follows a writing plan.
   1 Copy the writing plan (Table 1).
   2 Write notes in each space.
   3 Write a topic sentence for each paragraph.

Table 1: Writing plan

Introduction	
Problem	
Original solution	
Problems with the solution	
Invention: *what, who, when, etc.*	
Invention: *how it works*	
Conclusion	

C Study these pairs of sentences.
*There are many labour-saving devices in the modern
home. _____ devices save time and effort.*

*Clothes get dirty when you wear them. _____
problem was much worse in the past.*

   1 Which word is missing in each case?
   2 Read the Skills Check and check.
   3 Find and circle *this* and *these* in the essay
   opposite. If the noun is omitted, what does it
   refer to?

D Work in pairs. Read the sentence that comes
before each *this* or *these*. Can your partner
continue with the correct demonstrative and
something logical?

Skills Check

Using demonstratives to refer back

We know that we can use pronouns to refer back
to nouns or noun phrases.
Example:
*There are many labour-saving devices in the
modern home.* **They** *save time and effort.*
We can also use **this** or **these** + **the noun**. This
ensures that the reader understands what we are
referring to.
Example:
*There are many labour-saving devices in the modern
home.* **These (devices)** *save time and effort.*
We can sometimes omit the noun and just use
the demonstrative.

1 There are many labour-saving devices in the modern home. These devices save time and effort. _____, things were very different even a hundred years ago. All household chores had to be done by hand. The washing machine was one of the first labour-saving inventions that (a)_____.

2 Clothes get dirty _____ you wear them. This problem was much worse in the past, especially for people who (b) _____ _____ or lived in cities that (c)_____ or in rural areas that (d) _____.

3 Before washing machines were invented, clothes had to be washed by hand. _____ there was a river or stream in the area, the people could take the clothes to the water _____ hit them with a small rock _____ knock the dirt out. _____ they didn't live near running water, they had to get the water from a well _____ put the clothes in a bucket. Sometimes they used a washboard, which (e) _____ _____. They moved the clothes up and down the washboard _____ rub the dirt out.

4 There were three main drawbacks to this solution to the problem of washing clothes. Firstly, it took a long time _____ clean the clothes. Secondly, it was very hard work. Thirdly, clothes did not last very long _____ the stones _____ the washboard damaged them. A device was needed _____ speed up the process, _____ reduce the effort that (f) _____ and _____ look after the clothes.

In 1851, a man called James King, who (g) _____ 5 _____, invented a washing machine *powering / powered* by hand. People had to fill the machine, *carrying / carried* the water from a river or well, _____ they had to empty the machine, *using / used* buckets. This was still very hard work, _____ it did not take as long as before to clean the clothes. There were

various improvements to the design during the next 50 years. Then, in 1908, a company in Illinois, USA, produced the first washing machine *powering / powered* by electricity, which (h) _____ _____.

6 Modern washing machines normally use centrifugal force. This acts on objects when they _____ spin very fast. Washing machines contain six main components. These are: two drums, an electric motor, a pump, a heater and a computer. The clothes _____ put into the inner drum, which has holes in it. The washing cycle _____ programmed into the computer and the machine _____ switched on. Water _____ heated and pumped into the inner drum and this _____ then turned by the motor. The dirty clothes _____ pushed against the inside of the inner drum by centrifugal force. The water _____ pushed against the clothes and _____ tries to escape, but it must pass through the clothes. As the water _____ passes through the clothes, the dirt _____ carried away into the outer drum. The dirty water _____ then pumped out of the machine.

Lesson 4: Applying new skills

A Read the sentences in the blue box. They are adapted from the essay in Lessons 2 and 3.

1 What is the missing word or phrase in each case?

2 Read the Skills Check and check.

> **a** A hundred years ago, all household chores _____ by hand.
>
> **b** If people didn't live near running water, they _____ the water from a well.
>
> **c** People _____ James King's machine with water and they _____ the machine, using buckets.
>
> **d** The water is pushed against the clothes and it tries to escape, but it _____ through the clothes.

B Complete the names of the labour-saving devices in Table 1 with the correct vowel(s) in each space.

C Study the words in the yellow box.

1 Write the words next to the relevant device. You can use one word in two places.

2 Explain your choices.

> cook   cool   crease   dishes
> dust   filter   go off   grease
> heater   metal   suck   thermostat
> thermostat   timer   turn

D You are going to write about one of the labour-saving devices in Table 1 (right). You are going to use the same writing plan as the essay in Lesson 2.

1 Choose the device.

2 Copy the writing plan (Table 1 on page 32).

3 Do some research and make notes for each section.

4 Write a topic sentence for each paragraph.

5 Write your essay.

Table 1: Labour-saving devices

r __ fr __ g __ r __ t __ r	
__ l __ ctr __ c __ r __ n	
d __ shw __ sh __ r	
v __ c ____ m cl ____ n __ r	
m __ cr __ w __ v __ __ v __ n	

In this theme you are going to write about a famous novelist and his / her most famous novel.

Lesson 1: Vocabulary

You are going to learn some vocabulary to help you write the text.

A Write a short paragraph about the most famous novel from your culture. Use as many of the red words as possible.

B Imagine you are in the Faculty of Arts at Greenhill College. Read the information about your next assignment (below).

 1 Complete the assignment with a suitable word in each space.

 2 Listen to your tutor explaining the assignment and check your answers.

C You are going to write the first section of your assignment. You have researched the novelist and made notes (right).

 1 Turn the notes into short sentences.

 2 Organise your sentences into paragraphs.

 3 Join your sentences. Use each of the words and methods in the Skills Check Reminder.

 4 Write a first draft of this section of the essay.

ending *(n)*

setting *(n)*

source *(n)*

theme *(n)*

title *(n)*

translation *(n)*

background *(n)*

based on *(adj)*

childhood *(n)*

early life *(n)*

experience *(n and v)*

inspire *(v)*

novel *(n)*

novelist *(n)*

political *(adj)*

Greenhill College

Faculty of Arts

Charles Dickens is one of the most famous _____ in English literature, and *Oliver Twist* is one of his most famous books.

Assignment

Write a short essay about Dickens and *Oliver Twist* as follows:

Section 1: Dickens' _____ and _____ life, focusing on the _____ that _____ him to write *Oliver Twist*.

Section 2: Social and _____ events forming a _____ to the novel.

Section 3: A brief description of the plot of the _____.

D.O.B.	7/2/1812
Place	Portsmouth (naval town, S. coast Eng.)
Father	clerk (for navy)
Childhood / early life	2 family → London
	4 → Chatham (sm. town E. of L)
	4-12 = happy
	12 = f. → prison for debt;
	Ch. → out of school;
	→ work in factory
	13 = f. inherited money
	f. out of prison + Ch. → school
	15 → journalist;
	reporting at Courts of Law
	2/3 yrs later started to write fiction
	24 = published first novel
	25 = started 'Oliver Twist'
	= based on own exp. of poverty + knowledge of L. underworld

I experienced the life of poor children at first hand.

I reported on the trials of thieves and murderers and got to know the London underworld.

Skills Check

Reminder

Join short sentences into longer sentences with …

and / but / or / because / so / which / who

participles, e.g., *doing, did.*

Lesson 2: Writing

A Here is Section 1 of a student's assignment for the Faculty of Arts (Lesson 1). Write one linking word in each space.

Charles Dickens was born on 7th February, 1812, in Portsmouth, _____ is a naval town on the south coast of England. His father was a clerk _____ worked for the navy. Charles's family moved to London when he was two, then to Chatham, _____ is a small town to the east of London.

Charles had a happy childhood _____, when he was 12, his father was put into prison for debt. Charles was taken out of school _____ sent to work in a factory, where he experienced the life of poor children at first hand.

After a year, his father inherited a small amount of money _____ he could leave prison _____ Charles could return to school. When he was 15, he left school _____ become a journalist at the London Courts of Law, _____ on the trials of thieves and murderers and _____ to know the London underworld.

After a few years, he started to write fiction, _____ his first novel in 1836. The following year, he started 'Oliver Twist', _____ on his experiences of poverty _____ his knowledge of the criminal underworld of London.

B You are going to hear a short lecture to help with Section 2 of the assignment (Lesson 1). It is about the social and political background to Dickens's early life.
1 Listen to the lecture.
2 Summarise the information in one sentence.

C Here is the information from the lecture in short, simple sentences. Rewrite each group of sentences as one sentence.

1. *Oliver Twist* is the story of a boy. He is born in a workhouse. He is treated badly. He runs away at the age of nine. **Example:** *'Oliver Twist' is the story of a boy, born in a workhouse, who runs away at the age of nine because he is treated badly.*	5. The Poor Law set up buildings. They were called workhouses. They took in unemployed people. They took in orphaned children. They provided food and a bed in return for hard manual work.
2. He arrives in London. He gets involved with a group of thieves.	6. The government said that conditions in the workhouses must not be too comfortable. They wanted people to leave the workhouse as soon as possible.
3. Dickens was probably inspired to write the novel by a new law. It was called the Poor Law. It was passed in 1834. Dickens started work on the book three years later.	7. Many people in Britain did not agree with the Poor Law. Some of these people were rich. Many people in Britain did not agree with the basic idea that poor people were lazy.
4. The Poor Law was designed to help poor people. It was based on an idea. Some people thought people became poor because they were lazy.	8. Some rich people continued to help the poor. They gave money to beggars. Begging was illegal.

Lesson 3: Learning new skills

A What can you remember about Dickens's life?
How did his experiences inspire *Oliver Twist*?

B Study these pairs of sentences.

> *Charles's family moved to London.*
> *He was four **then**.*
> *Charles was sent to work in a factory.*
> *He experienced the life of poor children at first hand **there**.*

1 How can you join each pair into one sentence?

2 Read Skills Check 1.

3 Join the pairs of sentences in the yellow box in the same way.

a *Charles was born in Portsmouth. His father worked there.*

b *His father was put into prison for debt. He was 12 then.*

c *He left school. He was 15 then.*

d *Charles worked at the Courts of Law. He reported on trials there.*

e *Oliver ran away. He was nine then.*

C Study these two sentences.

> **a** *Some people thought that people became poor **because they were lazy**.*
> **b** *Some people thought that people became poor **because of their laziness**.*

1 What are the differences?

2 Read Skills Check 2.

3 Rewrite the sentences in the yellow box below so they are like sentence b above.

a *Dickens probably wrote 'Oliver Twist' because there was a new law.*

b *Did people become poor because they were lazy?*

c *Oliver runs away because he is treated badly.*

d *Dickens could write well about London criminals because he knew the underworld.*

e *Dickens believed that children often got involved in crime because they were poor.*

Lesson 4: Applying new skills

A Rewrite these phrases (*because* + verb) with *because of* + noun.

1 Because he was involved …
2 Because she designed …
3 Because they knew …
4 Because he inherited …
5 Because I was inspired …
6 Because you have experienced …
7 Because they treated …
8 Because I want …
9 Because we owe money …

B Rewrite these phrases (*because of* + noun) with *because* + adjective.

1 Because of his poverty …
2 Because of their laziness …
3 Because of my unemployment …
4 Because of her wealth …
5 Because of our comfort …

C Here is Section 3 of a student's assignment for the Faculty of Arts (Lesson 1).
Write one of the extra phrases from the yellow box in each space in the text.

> because of a man
> because of an inheritance
> because of his behaviour
> called Mr Brownlow
> committing his first crime
> orphaned at birth
> when he is nine
> where he looks after him
> where he meets Jack Dawkins
> who is the leader of a gang of thieves

D You are going to write an assignment.

1 Read the handout from the Faculty of Arts.
2 Choose a novelist and one of his / her novels.
3 Do some research and make notes of information for each section of the assignment.
4 Make a draft of each section.
5 Exchange drafts with a partner.
6 Indicate any problems with your partner's draft.
7 Write a final version.

Oliver Twist, _____,
grows up in the workhouse. One day, _____
_____, the other
boys make him ask for more soup.
_____, Mr. Bumble,
who runs the workhouse, sells Oliver to a local
undertaker, but Oliver runs away to London, _____
_____, who is
also nine. Jack takes him to Fagin, _____
_____. He trains Oliver in
picking pockets, but Oliver is caught _____
_____. However, the victim, an
elderly gentleman _____
_____, feels sorry for Oliver. He
takes him to his house, _____
_____. Oliver wants to stay
with Mr Brownlow for ever, but Fagin kidnaps him
_____ called Monks.
Oliver has many more adventures, then Mr Brownlow
discovers that Oliver is Monks's half brother and a
wealthy child _____
_____ from the father who he never knew.

Greenhill College

Faculty of Arts

Who is the most famous novelist in your culture? What is his or her most famous novel?

Assignment

Write a short essay about a novelist and his / her novel as follows:

Section 1: Childhood and early life, focusing on the experiences that inspired the novel.

Section 2: Social and / or political events that form a background to the novel.

Section 3: A brief description (300 words maximum) of the plot of the novel.

In this theme you are going to write about tourism in your country, using tables, graphs and charts.

athlete *(n)*

compete *(v)*

event *(n)*

gold medal *(n)*

point *(n)*

record *(n)*

score *(v)*

win *(v)*

winner *(n)*

attraction *(n)*

beach *(n)*

golf course *(n)*

heritage site *(n)*

museum *(n)*

statistic *(n)*

theme park *(n)*

tourism *(n)*

tourist *(n)*

trend *(n)*

wildlife *(n)*

zoo *(n)*

Lesson I: Vocabulary

You are going to learn some vocabulary that you will need to write about tourism.

A Look at the red words for 30 seconds. Then cover them and rewrite the words below, without the spelling mistakes.

1 atlete _____
2 compeet _____
3 efent _____
4 gold medle _____
5 piont _____
6 recod _____
7 skore _____
8 winer _____

B Who is the top athlete in your country? Write three sentences about the person, using some of the red words.

C Look at the pictures.
1 What do they all have in common?
2 Label each picture with a green word or phrase.

D Imagine you are a student in the Faculty of Sports and Leisure Management at Greenhill College. Complete the assignment information with a green word in each space.

E Write one or two sentences for each part of Section 1.

F Give your opinions in groups.
1 Is income from tourism in your country going up or down?
2 What are the most popular tourist attractions?
3 Where do most tourists come from?

Greenhill College

Faculty: Sports and Leisure Management
Topic: Tourism

Assignment

Do a survey of _____ in your own country.

1 Introduce your country briefly:
   1.1 location
   1.2 main geographic features
   1.3 climate
   1.4 history

2 Give recent _____ in the form of graphs and charts on:
   2.1 tourism income in recent years
   2.2 the most popular tourist _____, e.g., sandy _____, castles and other _____, museums, _____ parks
   2.3 where most _____ to your country come from

Give actual figures and describe _____, upwards or downwards.

Lesson 2: Writing

A Gina from Singapore has written about tourism in her country. Read some of her topic sentences in the yellow box.

    1 Complete each sentence with one word.

    2 What information do you expect to find in each paragraph?

B Read Gina's essay (page 41). Check your answers to Exercise A above.

C Gina has found a lot of extra information for Paragraphs 1 to 5.

    1 Find a suitable place in her essay for each piece of information in the blue box.

    2 Put a ⋀ sign with the letter of the extra information in each case.

    3 Change and / or add words to make the sentences link correctly.

D Complete Paragraphs 6 and 7 with the correct linking word in each space.

E Complete Paragraph 8 with suitable verbs. Put the verb into the correct form in each case.

Lesson 3: Learning new skills

A Which tourist attractions in Singapore would you like to visit?

B Read the Skills Check. Then look at the figures in the essay opposite.

    1 What does each figure show?

    2 What is the scale and unit of measurement for the line graph?

    3 What about the bar graph?

    4 What does *14%* in Figure 2 mean?

    5 What was the trend in tourism income from 1991 to 1995?

    6 What important information is missing from all the figures?

C You are going to hear Gina talking about the figures in her essay.

    1 Listen and make notes.

    2 Write a short paragraph about each figure.

---

1 Singapore is _____ in Southeast Asia.

2 The country has an _____ of about 640 square kilometres.

3 Since the _____ is tropical, it remains hot throughout the year.

4 The area has been _____ for at least 2,000 years.

5 In the 7th century, a Malayan empire was _____ on the island of Sumatra.

6 In the 13th _____, a prince arrived at the sandy shores of the main island.

7 Modern Singapore was _____ in 1819.

---

a Singapore consists of one main island and over 60 islets.

b The nature reserve contains many lakes.

c Singapore is linked to Malaysia by two bridges.

d It is situated just over a hundred kilometres north of the Equator.

e It is the highest point, at only 166 metres.

f Sumatra lies to the southwest of the country.

g The name means 'the island at the end of a peninsula'.

h They last from December to March and from June to September.

i Temasek became a prosperous outpost of the Malayan Empire.

Skills Check

Displaying statistics

There are several ways to display statistics. Choose the best way to help the reader understand the information.

Use ...	to show	Example
a table	**exact data**	
a line graph	**trends** over time	Figure 1
a pie chart	% **parts** of 1 item	Figure 2
a bar graph	**comparison**	Figure 3

Notes:

1 Give the **source** for all statistics.

2 Make sure your graphs have a clear **scale** and a **unit of measurement**.

1 Singapore is located in Southeast Asia. It is at the southern end of the Malay Peninsula. To the south, it is separated from Indonesia by the Singapore Strait.

2 The country has an area of about 640 square kilometres. The mainland is urban, but there is a large central nature reserve. The land is low-lying, rising to Bukit Timah.

3 Since the climate is tropical, it remains hot throughout the year. There are two rainy seasons. In addition, there are often thunderstorms in the afternoon or early evening.

4 The area has been inhabited for at least 2,000 years. The ancient Chinese called Singapore 'Pu-luo-chung'.

5 In the 7th century, a Malayan empire was established on the island of Sumatra. Singapore was called Temasek, or Sea Town, because of its location.

6 In the 13th century, a prince _____ was looking for a site for a new city, arrived at the sandy shores of the main island, _____ he glimpsed a strange animal. He was told it was a *singa*, _____ is the Sanskrit word for lion. In fact, it was almost certainly a tiger, but when the prince built his new city there, he called it *Singa pura*, _____ means Lion City.

7 Modern Singapore was founded in 1819 _____ the desire of the British for a trading post in the area. _____ the country gained its independence from Britain in 1959, it joined Malaya in 1963 to form Malaysia. _____, in 1965, Singapore became fully independent again. _____, Singapore has become one of the world's wealthiest countries.

8 Since independence, tourism has been an important sector of Singapore's economy. In 1984, a Tourism Task Force _____ to recommend ways _____ more visitors. It was decided _____ heritage sites and _____ Sentosa Island, which lies off the southern coast, as a resort, _____ museums, parks, golf courses, beaches and gardens. Safaris were started _____ the wildlife resources and theme-based centres _____, including Cinemania, Snow City and Volcanoland. In addition to its own tourist attractions, Singapore _____ a gateway for tourists to the rest of Southeast Asia, including Indonesia and Thailand.

Figure 1: Tourism income

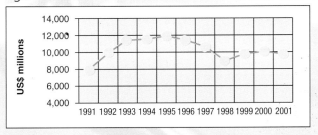

Figure 2: Tourist attractions by visits

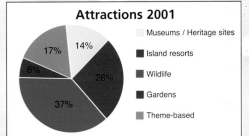

Figure 3: Tourist arrivals by country of origin

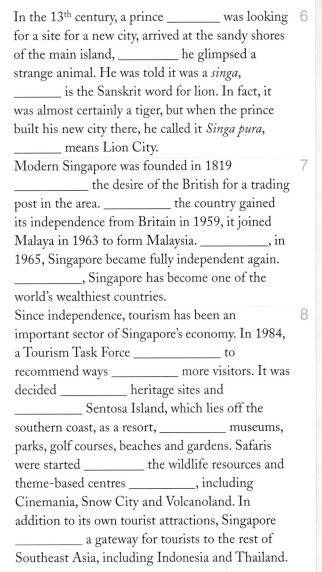
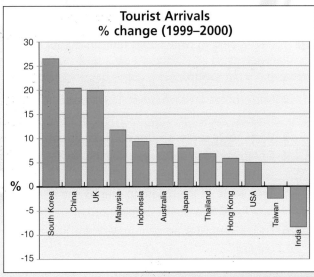

Lesson 4: Applying new skills

A Study these sentences from the essay in Lessons 2 and 3.

> **Since** the climate is tropical, it remains hot throughout the year.
> **Since** independence, tourism has been an important sector of Singapore's economy.

1 What does the word *since* mean in each case?
2 Read Skills Check 1 and check.
3 What does *since* mean in each sentence in the yellow box? Copy and complete each sentence logically. It doesn't have to be true!

B Read these sentences from Gina's essay describing the tourism figures. Copy and complete the sentences with words / phrases from Skills Check 2.

1 Figure 1 _____ the income from tourism from 1991 _____ 2001.
2 As you _____, income rose steadily at the beginning of this period, _____ a maximum of _____ under US$12 billion in 1995.
3 Then there was a decline _____ 1999.
4 Wildlife parks and safaris are clearly _____ popular, attracting more _____ five million people in 2001, _____ 37% of total visitors.
5 Figure 3 demonstrates the upward _____ in visitor numbers _____ 1999 and 2000.
6 As in _____ years, visitors from Indonesia formed the highest number, with a total of just over 1.3 million.
7 However, visitors from China showed _____ biggest percentage increase, _____ 21%.

C You are going to write about tourism in your own country.

1 Read the assignment again (Lesson 1).
2 Make notes on each point. Do research for the tourism statistics.
3 Write topic sentences for each paragraph.
4 Complete each paragraph, joining short sentences into longer ones.
5 Turn some of the data into graphs and charts (use Excel or a similar application).
6 Follow the usual procedure with drafting and editing.

Skills Check 1

Using *since*

The word **since** can mean: **because** or **in the period from** …

Use *since* to mean *in the period from* when the second part of the sentence is still true.

a Since Singapore is hot throughout the year, …
b Since Singapore is so close to Indonesia and Malaysia, …
c Since Singapore split from Malaysia in 1965, …
d Since the 13th century, …
e Since wildlife holidays are so popular, …

Skills Check 2

Describing graphs and charts

Graphs and charts give a picture of statistics, but you must still write about the information.

1	Refer to the correct figure	*Figure 1 shows / demonstrates …* *In Figure 2 you can see …*
2	Refer back	*As in previous years …*
3	Highlight key points	*As you can see, …* *As Figure 3 shows, …*
4	Round figures up and down	*just over / under US$12 billion* *more than five million visitors*
5	Give start points in time	*Since 1985, …* *Since then, …*
6	Give periods of time	*from 1991 to 2001* *between 1999 and 2000*
7	Give end points in time	*until 1999* *up to 1985*
8	Talk about movement up and down	*reach / rise to; decline / fall to* *up / down by 21%* *upward / downward trend*
9	Talk about levels	*maximum / minimum …* *the most / biggest / highest …*
10	Restate figures	*five million people,* *or 37% of total visitors*

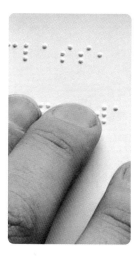  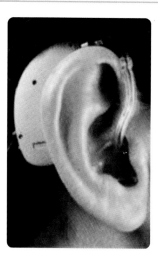

breakfast cereal (n)
calorie/s (n)
carbohydrate (n)
diet (n)
fat (n)
junk food (n)
protein (n)
access (n)
able-bodied (adj)
adapt (v)
adaptation (n)
blind (adj)
blindness (n)
deaf (adj)
deafness (n)
disability (n)
disabled (adj)
paralysed (adj)
paralysis (n)
partial/ly (adj/adv)

In this theme you are going to write about disabilities and access to education.

Lesson 1: Vocabulary

You are going to learn some vocabulary that you will need to write the essay.

Ⓐ Look at the red words.

1 Choose three of the words. Write one sentence for each to show the meaning.

2 Exchange sentences with a partner. Check grammar and spelling.

Ⓑ Complete these definitions with a green word in each case:

1 People who have normal function of all their senses are sometimes called _____.

2 People who do not have normal function of all their senses are _____.

3 People who can't see are _____.

4 People who can't hear are _____.

5 People who can't move are _____.

Ⓒ Cover the green words. Complete the table. Then uncover the green words and check your answers.

blind	
deaf	
disabled	
paralysed	

Ⓓ Look at the assignment – right.

1 Read and complete the assignment with a green word in each space. Make any necessary changes.

2 What is the main point of the text? Do you agree with it? Why (not)?

3 Brainstorm some answers to the two questions.

Greenhill College

Education Faculty

ASSIGNMENT 4: Access to Education

Education systems are designed for _____ students with no severe health problems. However, a large number of children in any society have some form of _____, like _____ blindness or total _____, or some kind of severe health problem, like diabetes. Education systems should not deny these students _____ to secondary and higher education. They should provide additional resources, and _____ courses to enable students to complete their studies.

Consider these questions

• What are some of the difficulties that _____ students have in an education system for able-bodied students?

• What _____ can schools and colleges make to their buildings and/or course programmes to provide better access?

Do some research in the library or on the Internet. Write a short essay answering the questions above.

Lesson 2: Writing review (1)

A In this course you have learnt to talk about graphs and charts.

Work in groups of three.

Student A: Look at Figure 1 opposite. **Student B:** Look at Figure 2 opposite.

Student C: Look at Figure 3 opposite.

1 Work out what your graph or chart shows. Don't worry if you don't understand all the words.

2 Close your books. Explain your graph or chart to the other two students in your group. Do a sketch to help with the explanation.

B Look at Figure 2. What sort of problem does each of the students below have?

Write your answers.

1 Zena cannot hear very well.	*Partial deafness.*
2 Suleiman cannot see at all.	
3 Paolo cannot speak very well.	
4 Donna needs a wheelchair.	
5 Eduardo has diabetes.	
6 Malcolm cannot remember things very well.	
7 Myrna get depressed sometimes.	
8 Asma cannot use her hands.	

C Look at Figure 3. What sort of disabilities would mean that a student needed each of the adaptations listed?

Example: Different exam formats –

A deaf student could not do a normal listening exam or oral test.

D Complete each sentence below with something suitable in the space provided.

1 *Figure 1 shows …*	
2 *In Figure 2 you can see …*	
3 *As Figure 3 shows, the most common course adaptation …*	
4 *Just over 75% of disabled students …*	
5 *Since 1986, the percentage of disabled students completing secondary school in the US …*	
6 *From 1986 to 2000, the gap between able-bodied and disabled students completing secondary school …*	
7 *The largest percentage of disabled students in the United States …*	
8 *Just under half of the colleges questioned said that they provided …*	

E Cover the first column above. Write a suitable opening to each sentence. Then uncover the column and check your ideas.

F Write one more sentence about the information in each figure.

Figure 1: Percentage of students completing secondary school

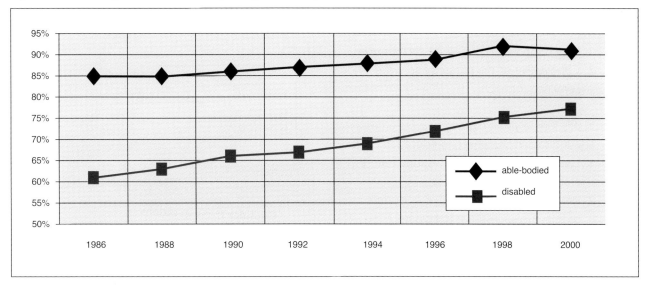

Figure 2: Breakdown of disabled college students by disability

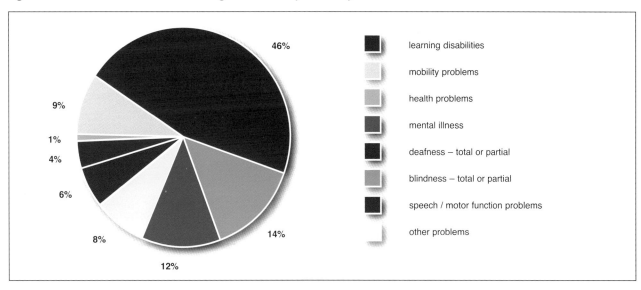

Figure 3: Course adaptations for disabled college students

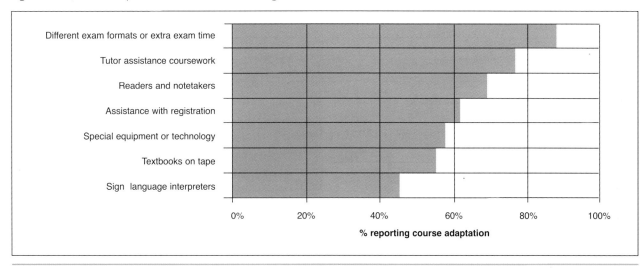

Lesson 3: Writing review (2)

A The words in the green box make phrases from the graphs in Lesson 2.
   1 Match the words and write each phrase.
   2 Choose five of the phrases and write a good sentence for each.

a	learning	assistance
b	mobility	blindness
c	able-bodied	disabilities
d	partial	equipment
e	tutor	function
f	special	language
g	sign	problems
h	motor	students

B In this theme you are going to write an essay about disabled students and education.
   1 Look again at the two questions from the assignment.
   2 Work in pairs. Look at Table 1. Write a problem in each space in column 2.

C Work in groups.
   1 Compare your tables from Exercise B.
   2 Put possible solutions to each problem in column 3. You can write about real products or you can invent new ones.

Consider these questions
- What are some of the difficulties that disabled students have in an education system for able-bodied students?
- What adaptations can schools and colleges make to their buildings and / or course programmes to provide better access for disabled students?

D Imagine that you have researched the questions and found the information opposite. Try to find a real solution from the research information for each problem in Table 1.

Table 1: Brainstorming and research

Disability	Problems in education	Solutions – own ideas	Solutions – from research
mobility problems	*can't get from car park to entrance*	*disabled parking near entrance;*	
blindness			
deafness			
speech problems			
motor function problems			

Braille is a system of writing for blind people, invented in the 19th century that uses combinations of six dots in a square.

Louis Braille was born in 1809 in a village near Paris. Braille, a French educator, was blinded by an accident when he was three years old. When he was 10, he was sent to a school for blind children, where he learnt a system of writing. It was very complicated, so he invented a better system that was easier to read and write. He explained his system in a book published in 1829.

Louise Braille died in 1852, but the system that he invented is still in use by blind people today.

In Braille, each character is represented by a pattern of dots in a square. There are six dots, numbered from the top 1, 2, 3 on the left and 4, 5, 6 on the right. For example, *a* is represented by dot 1 while *b* is dots 1 and 2. In the early days, an instrument shaped like a pencil was used (from the back of the paper) to raise one of the six dots and write Braille.

A new machine can turn graphs into 3D pictures that can be felt by blind people. This enables people with visual impairment to 'see' a picture of data, in a similar way to sighted people, but by touch rather than sight.

There are now keyboards for all kinds of disabilities. For example, for blind people there are keyboards with Braille symbols, which make a clicking sound when a key is pressed, while for deaf people there are keyboards with keys that light up on pressing. For those with motor disabilities, there are keyboards that can be operated by just one finger – in other words, there are no operations requiring multiple key pressings. You can set the keyboard to register only one symbol at each press, which helps users who find it difficult to make quick finger movements. With normal keyboards, holding a key down for more than a millisecond results in multiple symbols being produced.

All of these keyboards plug into the normal keyboard socket on a computer.

Braille 'n Talk is a new computer software program from Enable.com. The program comes with a special keyboard with six keys. When a key is pressed, the computer speaks the letter back to the user. When a series of characters is typed to make a word, the computer speaks that word. It can also speak whole sentences.

Brenda Shaw, who is partially blind, is delighted with the new programme.

'Before Braille 'n Talk I had no way of knowing what I had typed,' she says. 'With this programme, I proofread my work and correct it.'

Deaf people often learn lip-reading in childhood, but this method is only useful when the speaker talks directly to the deaf person. When he or she turns away, lip-reading is impossible. This means that the method cannot normally be used by the deaf in a lecture room, since the lecturer often turns away, perhaps to write on the board or point to an illustration while talking about it. However, lecturers can now wear a web cam focussed on the lips at all times. The image is transmitted to an intranet system, which means that students logged on to the system can read the lecturer's lips throughout the lecture.

Most people with hearing difficulties are not actually deaf. They simply cannot hear as well as other people. Hearing aids in the ear work very well for these people in normal conversation, but they do not work properly in large halls. The solution is a microphone and a loop, carrying the signal around the room. It is picked up by hearing aids with telecoils (or T-coils). It sounds as if the speaker is talking directly into the listener's ear.

Many lecture rooms and other public places are now fitted with listening loops. If you have a hearing aid with a T-coil, look for the sign reading 'Turn your aid to the T position.'

People who have severe motor function problems cannot communicate easily with people. Voice synthesisers enable these people to operate computers and, in this way, produce speech at almost the same speed as able-bodied speakers. This technology uses a switch that can be operated by movement of any sort – even sucking or blowing through a straw.

Lesson 4: Writing review (3)

A You will need many different sentence patterns for your assignment. In this course you have studied the patterns below. There are **two** mistakes in each pattern – extra word, missing word, wrong word or wrong word order. Find the mistakes and correct them.

1 To sum, it seems that both heredity and environment has an effect on appearance, personality, likes and dislikes.

2 John Locke, was a British philosopher of the 17th century, believes that a baby is like a clean sheet of paper.

3 The applications evaluated for qualifications and experiences.

4 To discovering the correct size of radiator for a particular room, you must to calculate the volume of the room.

5 Generally speaking, you can heat a kitchen less other rooms because of there will often be extra heat from cooking.

6 Bathrooms, on the other hand, need most heating, because a bathroom of the same size needs a radiator with an output of 2 kW.

7 If there will be draughts, you will lose a lot of heat and wasting energy.

8 The country produces around 350,000 kilos per annum, which just over a third of world produce of gold.

9 Greek and Roman advances rediscovered by Arabs, which translated a lot of the ancient learning.

10 It have been 26 or 27 civilizations begun with the Egyptian.

11 The new cheap books spreaded the knowledge of earlier civilizations, translating in many cases by Arab scholars.

12 There is many labour-saving devices in the modern home. This save time and money.

13 Dickens's family were moved to Chatham when he was four then.

14 Charles sent to work in a factory, where he experienced the life of poor children at first hand there.

B Complete these sentences. They are all about disability and access to education. They use some of the patterns from Exercise A.

1 To sum up, it seems that there are many devices …

2 The lecturer's voice is picked up by a microphone and …

3 To hear the lecturer's voice on the listening loop, you must …

4 Generally speaking, disabled students have problems in higher education because …

5 If we remove the problems of access to education, people with disabilities …

C You must choose a writing plan for your essay. Look at the two writing plans. Which is better? Why?

D Write your essay. Try to use some of the new sentence patterns that you have studied in this course.

1 Write a topic sentence for each paragraph of the main body.

2 Add extra sentences to each paragraph.

3 Add an introduction and conclusion.

4 Exchange drafts, etc.

Plan 1:
Introduction
Problems of disabled students
Solutions to the problems
Conclusion

Plan 2:
Introduction
Problem 1 of disabled students
Solution 1
Problem 2, etc.
Conclusion

THEME 1
Education, What's Your Learning Style?

doubled (adj)

link (v)

multiple (adj)

open (adj)

organise (v)

practice (n)

relevant (adj)

revise (v)

silent (adj)

function (n)

grammar (n)

language (n)

listening (n)

pronunciation (n)

reading (n)

speaking (n)

vocabulary (n)

writing (n)

THEME 2
Daily Life, What Made Me ... Me?

adult (n)

decision (n)

parent (n)

teenager (n)

affect (v)

appearance (n)

effect (n)

environment (n)

factor (n)

heredity (n)

personality (n)

theory (n)

THEME 3
Work and Business, Hiring and Firing

administrator (n)

conclude (v)

equipment (n)

furniture (n)

purchase (v)

recommendation (n)

report (n)

resource (n)

action (n)

advertise (v)

appoint (v)

decision (n)

experience (n)

process (n)

qualification (n)

recruitment (n)

reference (n)

reject (v)

THEME 4
Science and Nature, Heating and Cooling

achieve (v)

aim (n)

construct (v)

facts and figures (n)

fresh (water) (adj)

project (n)

structure (n)

calculate (v)

cool (v)

energy (n)

gain (v)

heat (v)

insulate (v)

insulated (adj)

insulation (n)

lose (v)

waste (v)

THEME 5
The Physical World, Extraction Industries

agriculture (n)

area (n)

border (n)

climate (n)

continent (n)

industry (n)

location (n)

main (adj)

population (n)

extraction (n)

fossil fuel (n)

metal (n)

mine (v)

mining (n)

petroleum (n)

producer (n)

product (n)

THEME 6
Culture and Civilization, The Civilization Still Flourishes

bride (n)

ceremony (ies) (n)

engagement (n)

groom (n)

marriage (n)

married (adj)

wedding (n)

advance (n)

architecture (n)

flourish (v)

law (n)

relate (to) (v)

the arts (n)

THEME 7
They Made Our World, Labour-Saving Devices

decide (v)

develop (v)

produce (v)

reach (v)

realise (v)

sell (v)

solve (v)

think (of) (v)

work (v) (= do the job correctly)

appliance (n)

device (n)

dishwasher (n)

electric iron (n)

labour-saving (adj)

microwave oven (n)

refrigerator (n)

vacuum cleaner (n)

washing machine (n)

THEME 8
Art and Literature, Novelists and Their Novels

ending (n)

setting (n)

source (n)

theme (n)

title (n)

translation (n)

background (n)

based on (adj)

childhood (n)

early life (n)

experience (n and v)

inspire (v)

novel (n)

novelist (n)

political (adj)

THEME 9
Sports and Leisure,
As Figure 1 Shows ...

athlete *(n)*

compete *(v)*

event *(n)*

gold medal *(n)*

point *(n)*

record *(n)*

score *(v)*

win *(v)*

winner *(n)*

attraction *(n)*

beach *(n)*

golf course *(n)*

heritage site *(n)*

museum *(n)*

statistic *(n)*

theme park *(n)*

tourism *(n)*

tourist *(n)*

trend *(n)*

wildlife *(n)*

zoo *(n)*

THEME 10
Nutrition and Health,
Education for Everybody

breakfast cereal *(n)*

calorie/s *(n)*

carbohydrate *(n)*

diet *(n)*

fat *(n)*

junk food *(n)*

protein *(n)*

access *(n)*

able-bodied *(adj)*

adapt *(v)*

adaptation *(n)*

blind *(adj)*

blindness *(n)*

deaf *(adj)*

deafness *(n)*

disability *(n)*

disabled *(adj)*

paralysed *(adj)*

paralysis *(n)*

partial/ly *(adj/adv)*

able-bodied *(adj)*

access *(n)*

achieve *(v)*

action *(n)*

adapt *(v)*

adaptation *(n)*

administrator *(n)*

adult *(n)*

advance *(n)*

advertise *(v)*

affect *(v)*

agriculture *(n)*

aim *(n)*

appearance *(n)*

appliance *(n)*

appoint *(v)*

architecture *(n)*

area *(n)*

athlete *(n)*

attraction *(n)*

background *(n)*

based on *(adj)*

beach *(n)*

blind *(adj)*

blindness *(n)*

border *(n)*

breakfast cereal *(n)*

bride *(n)*

calculate *(v)*

calorie/s *(n)*

carbohydrate *(n)*

ceremony (ies) *(n)*

childhood *(n)*

climate *(n)*

compete *(v)*

conclude *(v)*

construct *(v)*

continent *(n)*

cool *(v)*

deaf *(adj)*

deafness *(n)*

decide *(v)*

decision *(n)*

decision *(n)*

develop *(v)*

device *(n)*

diet *(n)*

disability *(n)*

disabled *(adj)*

dishwasher *(n)*

doubled *(adj)*

early life *(n)*

effect *(n)*

electric iron *(n)*

ending *(n)*

energy *(n)*

engagement *(n)*

environment *(n)*

equipment (n)

event (n)

experience (n and v)

extraction (n)

factor (n)

facts and figures (n)

fat (n)

flourish (v)

fossil fuel (n)

fresh (water) (adj)

function (n)

furniture (n)

gain (v)

gold medal (n)

golf course (n)

grammar (n)

groom (n)

heat (v)

heredity (n)

heritage site (n)

industry (n)

inspire (v)

insulate (v)

insulated (adj)

insulation (n)

junk food (n)

labour-saving (adj)

language (n)

law (n)

link (v)

listening (n)

location (n)

lose (v)

main (adj)

marriage (n)

married (adj)

metal (n)

microwave oven (n)

mine (v)

mining (n)

multiple (adj)

museum (n)

novel (n)

novelist (n)

open (adj)

organize (v)

paralysed (adj)

paralysis (n)

parent (n)

partial/ly
(adj and adv)

personality (n)

petroleum (n)

point (n)

political (adj)

population (n)

practice (n)

process (n)

produce (v)

producer (n)

product (n)

project (n)

pronunciation (n)

protein (n)

purchase (v)

qualification (n)

reach (v)

reading (n)

realise (v)

recommendation (n)

record (n)

recruitment (n)

reference (n)

refrigerator (n)

reject (v)

relate (to) (v)

relevant (adj)

report (n)

resource (n)

revise (v)

score (v)

sell (v)

setting (n)

silent (adj)

solve (v)

source (n)

speaking (n)

statistic (n)

structure (n)

teenager (n)

the arts (n)

theme (n)

theme park (n)

theory (n)

think (of) (v)

title (n)

tourism (n)

tourist (n)

translation (n)

trend (n)

vacuum cleaner (n)

vocabulary (n)

washing machine (n)

waste (v)

wedding (n)

wildlife (n)

win (v)

winner (n)

work (v) (= do the job correctly)

writing (n)

zoo (n)